MARTIN
LUTHER
FATHER OF THE REFORMATION

SPECIAL LIVES IN HISTORY THAT BECOME

Signature LIVES

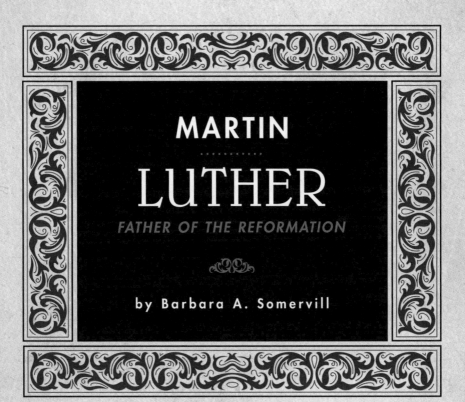

MARTIN
LUTHER
FATHER OF THE REFORMATION

by Barbara A. Somervill

Content Adviser: James F. Korthals,
Professor of Church History,
Wisconsin Lutheran Seminary

Reading Adviser: Rosemary G. Palmer, Ph.D.,
Department of Literacy, College of Education,
Boise State University

COMPASS POINT BOOKS MINNEAPOLIS, MINNESOTA

Compass Point Books
3109 West 50th Street, #115
Minneapolis, MN 55410

Visit Compass Point Books on the Internet at *www.compasspointbooks.com*
or e-mail your request to *custserv@compasspointbooks.com*

Editor: Sue Vander Hook
Page Production: Heather Griffin, Bobbie Nuytten
Photo Researcher: Svetlana Zhurkin
Cartographer: XNR Productions, Inc.
Library Consultant: Kathleen Baxter

Art Director: Jaime Martens
Creative Director: Keith Griffin
Editorial Director: Carol Jones
Managing Editor: Catherine Neitge

Library of Congress Cataloging-in-Publication Data
Somervill, Barbara A.
  Martin Luther: Father of the Reformation / by Barbara A. Somervill
  p. cm—(Signature lives)
  Includes bibliographical references and index.
ISBN 0-7565-1593-9 (hardcover)
  1. Luther, Martin, 1483–1546—Juvenile literature. 2. Reformers—
Germany—Biography—Juvenile literature. 3. Reformation—Germany—
Juvenile literature. 4. Lutheran Church—Germany—Clergy—Biography—
Juvenile literature. I. Title. II. Series.
  BR325.S66 2006
  284.1092—dc22   2005025212

Signature Lives

REFORMATION ERA

The winds of change howled through Europe during the 1500s. The continent that had been united by the Catholic Church found itself in an uproar. In an attempt to reform the church, some people left the established religion, while others worked from within. The changes that began in Germany in 1517 when Martin Luther wrote his *Ninety-Five Theses* would transform everything. The Protestant Reformation's impact would be felt in all aspects of life—at home, in government, and in economics. Straddling the Middle Ages and the Renaissance, the Protestant Reformation would change the church, religion, and the world itself.

Table of Contents

1 "I Cannot and Will Not Retract"

ↄ৯৴৵৩

Power, greed, and religious conflict hovered over Europe like a dark cloud. It was the early 1500s. People were burned at the stake for their faith, while others had religious experiences in gloomy towers. People claimed revelations from God and told of encounters with the devil.

Bolts of lightning and crashes of thunder drove one man in particular to Christian service. On a hot, muggy day in July 1505, a storm raged as law student Martin Luther walked to the University of Erfurt in Germany. As rain beat on him and lightning struck nearby, he cried out in fear:

St. Anne, help me! I will become a monk.

Martin Luther painting by Lucas Cranach, the Elder (1472–1553)

The storm passed by, and Luther kept his promise. He dropped out of school and entered a monastery. Later he would challenge the church that taught him, housed him, and made him a priest. He would speak out against the most powerful religious and political establishment of the time—the Catholic Church.

This era came to be known as the Protestant Reformation, a time when people protested in order to bring about reform, or change. It revolved around Luther, but appeals for religious reform had echoed throughout the Christian world long before. In the

Pope Gregory VII (1020–1085) encouraged reform in the Catholic Church.

11th century, Pope Gregory VII tried to improve the Catholic Church and correct the wrongs that had occurred. In 1215, Pope Innocent III wanted to change the church and make it stronger.

Nicholas of Cusa, a German priest, openly criticized the pope, the supreme leader of the Catholic Church, and other religious leaders in the 1450s. He claimed, "It is the pope and the cardinals who daily commit the most fearful transgression [sin] and abuses." Desiderius

Erasmus, a well-known scholar of the early 1500s, asked the church to change. He claimed that the official Bible of the Catholic Church—the Latin Vulgate—had thousands of errors.

For centuries, the Catholic Church had provided many people with stability, peace, and security. It had offered strong religious leadership through the pope as well as the cardinals and bishops that served under him. But people throughout the years had asked the church to make changes. Reform had been the topic of discussion at every religious conference of the Catholic Church between 1378 and 1514.

Desiderius Erasmus (c. 1469–1536) tried to change the Catholic Church from within.

Martin Luther also wanted the church to change. About 12 years after he entered the monastery, he wrote down his complaints—95 of them, to be exact—against the Catholic Church. On October 31, 1517, he nailed them to the door of the Castle Church in Wittenberg, Germany. It was a common place to post questions that would encourage discussion among students and faculty at the University of

Wittenberg. But Luther's *Ninety-Five Theses*, as they came to be called, sparked more than discussion. They were written in Latin, but someone translated them into German. Thousands of copies were printed and distributed throughout Germany. A fire of reform was lit that was different from any before. Luther's list challenged what he thought the church was doing wrong. He also questioned church doctrine—its core religious beliefs.

The Catholic Church considered Luther's claims to be heresy—defying the church. It was a crime

In 1517, when Martin Luther nailed his Ninety-Five Theses to the door of the Castle Church in Wittenberg, Germany, he didn't realize that his ideas would change religion and alter the course of history.

that could lead to torture, prison, or even death. But convicting and punishing this priest and professor would not happen easily. Luther would stand before political and religious leaders several times to defend his beliefs.

At Worms, Germany, in 1521, Luther stood before the most powerful leaders of the Holy Roman Empire. The emperor, the princes of Germany, the military, and top leaders of the Catholic Church were there. Piled high before him was the evidence—the books he had written. The examiner, a representative of the church, asked whether he had written them. "The books are all mine, and I have written more," he admitted in a voice that was barely heard.

The second question was more difficult. Did he still believe what the books taught, and was there a part of them he would now choose to recant, or take back? Luther replied, "This affects the salvation of souls. ... I beg you, give me time." The emperor granted him one day to answer.

The next day, in a hot, crowded room, the examiner again questioned Luther. Would he recant these books and the errors they contained? Luther addressed his accusers, probably to avoid giving a direct answer. He said he had written three types of books. Some taught about Christian faith; others attacked the pope and his teachings; and the rest attacked individuals who supported the pope.

Martin Luther defended himself before Emperor Charles V at the Diet of Worms in 1521.

The examiner again pressed him to tell the crowd whether he would take back what he had written. Luther answered:

> *Unless I am proved wrong by the testimony of Scriptures or by evident reason I am bound in conscience and held fast to the Word of God ... I cannot and will not retract anything, for it is neither safe nor salutary [valuable] to act against one's conscience.*

According to tradition, Luther added, "Here I stand. I can do no other. God help me! Amen." The people packed in the crowded room burst into an uproar. The emperor left the room. Luther's supporters celebrated, while others demanded that he be declared a heretic and an outlaw.

Luther left Worms and headed back to Wittenberg with his friend Nicholas Amsdorf. Several other friends accompanied them, but the group never arrived at Wittenberg. Along the way, five armed and masked horsemen approached them in the deep woods. Luther wasn't alarmed. He whispered to Amsdorf that they were among friends. The kidnapping had been staged to protect Luther.

That night, Luther's would-be captors took him to the Wartburg Castle near Eisenach, Germany. He remained there in hiding for almost 10 months, disguised as a knight named *Junker Jörg* (Knight George). He was fed, clothed, and protected. During his stay, he studied the Bible, wrote, and translated the New Testament portion of the Bible into German.

While he was there, his ideas quickly spread throughout Europe, sometimes with a force that even Luther couldn't understand or control. He had not planned to start a revolution. He never intended his *Ninety-Five Theses* to stir up so much controversy or conflict. But his beliefs would end up changing religion and altering the course of history. They would also divide the Catholic Church forever. ❧

2 HARD TIMES

❧❧❧❧

On November 10, 1483, Margarethe Lindemann Luder gave birth to a son. Among Catholics, it was customary to baptize babies as soon as possible. Six out of 10 children died as infants at that time, so parents promptly fulfilled this religious practice. They believed baptism would secure their babies' places in heaven.

On November 11, Hans Luder took his hours-old son to Sts. Peter and Paul Church, where a priest baptized him. That day was also a Catholic holy day, the feast of St. Martin de Tours. Hans and Margarethe followed another custom and named their son after this fourth-century Catholic bishop. As holy water was poured over the baby's head, he was christened, or named, Martin.

Martin Luther was born in Eisleben, Germany, on November 10, 1483.

*Hans Luder
(1459–1530),
Martin Luther's
father*

Before Martin was 1 year old, the Luders (later called Luthers) gathered up their belongings and moved about 10 miles (16 kilometers) away to Mansfeld. It was closer to the hills, where Hans took a job mining copper.

A miner's work was difficult and dangerous. It was no wonder miners had their own saint—St. Anne—to whom they prayed for protection. Hans was a hard worker and a determined man, who would one day own six mine shafts and two plants where copper was smelted. He also held a respected position on Mansfeld's city council.

The Luthers were strict, religious parents. They expected Martin and the six other children who would come after him to do what was right. Martin later remembered how his mother beat him until his hands bled for stealing a nut. His father once whipped him severely for playing a joke on someone.

The late 1400s was not an easy time to raise a family. Although some people were producing great works of art and discovering new worlds across an uncharted ocean, others were struggling to stay alive. Thousands had died from the bubonic plague, a deadly disease that affected lymph glands and turned skin a blackish color. It came to be called the Black Death. Those who managed to survive struggled to get enough to eat and to find clean water. Beggars were an everyday sight, and crime was commonplace.

Margarethe Luder (1460–1531), Martin Luther's mother

In the midst of personal storms, the Catholic Church offered hope. But religion also brought with it fear and dread. People commonly believed in the devil, evil spirits, and witches. They thought netherworld creatures lurked in the hills and around every corner. Martin believed that a hill called Pubelsberg was the home of captive devils, and he told of witches who lived in Prussia and Lapland.

People also feared God, whom they believed to be stern and judgmental. They dreaded the punishment they thought they deserved for their sins. The Catholic Church taught that penance, or acts that proved people were sorry for their sins, would release them from God's eternal punishment. As a result, they performed many virtuous deeds.

Catholics often went on pilgrimages, or journeys to places considered holy, such as shrines or churches. Sometimes they intentionally lived a life of poverty to work off their penalties. They fervently prayed to saints and visited churches that housed sacred items in hope that God's punishment upon them would be reduced. They journeyed many miles to view relics such as a bone or hair of a saint or a splinter from the cross of Jesus Christ. Catholics believed they should do whatever they could to shorten their time in purgatory, the place they believed souls of the dead went until payment was made for the penalty of their sins.

> *Since the first century, Christians have gone on pilgrimages to sites connected with the birth, life, and crucifixion of Jesus. Today, many Christians visit the Holy Land (present-day Israel) or Rome, Italy (center of the Roman Catholic Church). On April 2, 2005, about 4 million people traveled to Rome and joined 3 million already living there to see the body of Pope John Paul II lie in state.*

Church members could also purchase an indulgence, an official document signed by the pope that was said to shorten a person's time in purgatory. On the blank line, people could write their own names or the names of loved ones. The price of an indulgence was based on a person's income.

The Luthers lived in an entirely Catholic culture.

Their lives, like those of other citizens of the Holy Roman Empire, revolved around the church. Hans made sure Martin participated in Mass and received an education at a church-run school in Mansfeld.

Martin learned to read and write Latin, the language of scholars and the language used by the Catholic Church. He also studied music and grammar, and memorized passages from the Bible. The teachers were stern and expected students to complete their lessons or suffer the consequences. Martin grew up fearing those penalties. One morning, he was struck 15 times for not mastering his Latin grammar.

In 1497, at the age of 13, Martin went to Magdeburg, about 60 miles (95 km) from Eisleben, to attend a boarding school run by the Brethren

Hans Luther made sure his son Martin received a good education.

of the Common Life. It was an extremely religious organization, although it was not connected with the Catholic Church. The Brethren lived a simple life of prayer, religious readings, and Bible study. Music was an important part of their education. Students often went about Magdeburg singing, gladly accepting money, food, or drink along the way.

Martin was at Magdeburg just one year when his father sent him to St. George's Latin school in Eisenach for three years. He was a good student, and in 1501,

Young Martin Luther and his school companions sang for Magdeburg residents at their homes.

probably upon the recommendation of his teachers, he began studying at the University of Erfurt. His father paid for his tuition, which was something most people of his social status couldn't do. But Hans had worked his way up in the copper mining industry and could afford to pay for his son's education. After all, if Martin became a lawyer or judge, he would be able to care for his aging parents.

At the university, Martin lived in a building called a bursa, where he slept, ate, and studied under the supervision of the master of the house. The students followed a rigid schedule. Early morning worship and prayers were followed by the first meal of the day, a religious service, and classes. Martin moved quickly through the required courses and earned a bachelor's degree in one year, just before his 19th birthday. Three years later, he earned his master's degree and could go on to pursue a professional degree.

The university had three choices—law, medicine, or theology. Theology, the study of religion, was considered the most honorable of all. But Hans wanted Martin to become a lawyer. Martin obeyed his father and began studying law in May 1505.

That summer, in the midst of a thunderstorm, the course of his life changed. He would never become a lawyer nor support his aging parents. But his decision to become a Catholic monk would dramatically change his life and alter the course of history. ✿

3 MONK OF THE BLACK CLOISTER

❦

In July 1505, 21-year-old Martin Luther celebrated with several friends before giving up the university classroom for a monastery. He knocked on a monastery door in Erfurt and asked to be taken in. He told his friends, "This day you see me, and then, not ever again."

There were several monasteries to choose from in Erfurt. Some were called Dominican and some Franciscan, according to which saint they followed. But Luther chose the Augustinians, the monks who followed St. Augustine, a fifth-century Catholic scholar and bishop. They shunned the luxuries of the outside world and sought to fulfill their religious vows to God.

Monastery life demanded strict obedience to the

In 1505, Martin Luther entered the Augustinian monastery in Erfurt, Germany, to become a Catholic monk.

A nearly shaved head showed that a monk had given up worldly fashion and pleasures.

rules of the order, or organization. As was customary for monks, Luther received a tonsure, the shaving of his head except for a horizontal ring of hair. The monks lived a life of self-discipline, self-punishment, and nearly constant prayer. Luther and his fellow monks began the daily routine when bells sounded at 2 A.M. for the first prayers of the day. They prayed seven more times each day. Their schedule also included meditation, Bible study, and two meals. Each monk was assigned a proctor, someone who guided and evaluated his spiritual progress.

Luther was an enthusiastic monk. He eagerly pursued what he thought would bring him closer to God and free him from his fears and guilt. At least daily and sometimes more often, Luther confessed his sins to a priest. He was taught how important it was to include every sin, even wrong motives or thoughts. He often left confession still feeling guilty and unworthy of God's love. He detested this time, since he could always think of one more sin that he had forgotten.

Penance followed confession. Monks often denied themselves food, drink, sleep, or warmth for long periods of time to prove how sorry they were. But although Luther did everything he was taught, he constantly doubted that God would accept him. He never felt quite holy enough for a holy God.

Johann von Staupitz, head of the Augustinian order, often worried about Luther. In order to keep this very serious monk busy, von Staupitz ordered him to study to become a priest. In 1507, just about

Luther spent most of his time in prayer, Bible study, and confession as he sought to be accepted by God.

a year and a half after he entered the monastery, 23-year-old Luther was ordained a Catholic priest. One of his most sacred duties was to celebrate Mass, a Catholic church service and a sacred ceremony.

On the day of Luther's first Mass, bells chimed, and monks chanted. Dressed in a special robe adorned with bells and surrounded by incense and candles, Luther stood by the altar and spoke. According to church doctrine, his words of consecration miraculously turned the bread into the body of Christ, and the wine became Christ's blood. Luther later admitted that he was so terror-stricken by this experience that he almost ran away from the altar. "Who am I," he said, "that I should lift up mine eyes or raise my hands to the divine Majesty?"

Luther had invited his father to come that day. They hadn't seen each other since he entered the monastery. But now, accompanied by 20 horsemen, Hans had arrived at his son's first Mass. He made a generous donation to the monastery and celebrated with his son at the banquet that followed. But when Martin asked his father why he had been against his becoming a monk, Hans became angry. He replied:

> *You learned scholar, have you never read in the Bible that you should honor your father and your mother? And here you have left me and your dear mother to look after ourselves in our old age.*

Luther said he would pray for his parents' souls.

Luther turned to von Staupitz for counsel and guidance. In many ways, von Staupitz served as his role model and a sort of father. In 1508, von Staupitz sent 25-year-old Luther to the University of Wittenberg to teach a course. It was a new university, started by Frederick the Wise of Saxony in 1502. Frederick was an elector, one of the seven princes of the Holy Roman Empire, who elected the emperor. Frederick needed teachers and welcomed anyone recommended by von Staupitz.

Johann von Staupitz (1465–1524) was Luther's superior as well as his mentor.

About 2,000 people lived in Wittenberg, a small town in northeastern Germany. Its main industry was brewing beer, much of which they consumed. The town market, described by some as a mudhole, was the center of drinking and fighting. The university, like most schools at the time, had close ties to the Catholic Church. Since it was still under construction, some classes were held in the local monastery, while others met in a 14th-century castle in town.

Luther's time at Wittenberg was filled with spiritual doubts. He constantly questioned his standing with God and the teachings of the Catholic Church. Later he would recall:

> *The name of Christ often frightened me, and when I looked on Him and the cross, He seemed to me like a flash of lightning. When people mentioned His name, I would rather have heard the devil mentioned. For I believed that I would have to do good works until they made Christ love and forgive me.*

Luther's uncertainties tormented him. He tried very hard to be holy, but he constantly told himself that he was not.

When he finished teaching the one-term course, Luther returned to Erfurt. He also returned to conflicts among the Augustinians. Nearly 100 years before, the order had divided. On one side were the monks who wanted to obey every rule. They became known as the Observant Augustinians. The others thought the order should be less strict. They were called the Conventual Augustinians. Von Staupitz was trying to get the groups to come together again. But he met with resistance. The issue became serious. The Observant Augustinians decided to resist the decisions made by von Staupitz and his superiors.

The Observants chose a representative to appeal

to top leaders of the Catholic Church in Rome, Italy. Since monks never traveled alone, Luther was asked to accompany him. In November 1510, Luther and the other monk set out on foot for Rome, where the

Luther was afraid of Jesus, because he felt unworthy of His love and forgiveness.

pope lived. Their 850-mile (1,360-km) trek across the Alps during a particularly harsh winter was cold and bitter. They stopped at monasteries along the way for food and lodging.

Forty days later, the two monks arrived in Rome, and Luther was suddenly plunged into a world he had never experienced. It was the center of the institution to which he had dedicated his entire life. At the first sight of the holy city, he threw himself on the ground and said, "How blessed are you, Holy Rome!"

Rome was a storehouse of sacred relics. Certain relics selected by Pope Leo X were so sacred that simply viewing them and paying the price of some gold coins was said to reduce a person's time in purgatory by up to 4,000 years, it was said. At one tomb in Rome were the bodies of 40 popes, 76,000 martyrs, and what was said to be a piece of Moses' burning bush. Rome also had sacred portraits, chains, scissors, hair, stones, coins, and other religious artifacts. Rome even claimed to have the entire bodies of St. Peter and St. Paul, two of the early followers of Jesus. The bodies

In 1929, the center for the Roman Catholic Church in Rome, Italy, became an independent state called Vatican City. It is the site of the pope's residence, St. Peter's Basilica, and the Sistine Chapel. In July 2004, Vatican City gained full membership in the United Nations. However, it chose not to have voting rights. Vatican City is the smallest state in the world. It has its own post office, bank, supermarket, electric plant, and railway station.

had been divided to share the benefits. The heads were at the Lateran Palace where the pope lived, and each of four churches received half of a body.

A sacred object that was said to be a nail from the cross of Jesus is magnificently displayed.

Thousands of pilgrims flocked to Rome to see these sacred items or to pray or participate in Mass at holy churches and sacred shrines.

Above all, Rome had the *Santa Scala*—the Sacred Stairs. They were said to be the very steps that Christ climbed in Jerusalem when he was questioned by Pontius Pilate. As the story went, they were brought to Rome and rebuilt at the Lateran Palace.

The Sacred Stairs in front of the Lateran Palace in Rome, Italy

Luther was prepared to take advantage of every spiritual benefit available to him in the city. He went to confession and celebrated Mass at holy sites. He visited the catacombs where early Christians were buried and paid homage to the bones of dead saints and holy relics. So passionate was he for this holy place, he said, that he ran through the sacred places "like a mad ... saint."

But as much as he was in awe of Rome, he soon became disenchanted. He was not impressed with the religious leaders. In fact, he thought they were ignorant of the Bible, lazy, and lacking in moral goodness and dedication. He observed them as they rushed through Mass. Then they told Luther to *"Passa! Passa!"*—"Get a move on!"—when he was just beginning to celebrate his own Mass.

To Luther, the priests of Rome were more interested in comfort and fine dining than in prayer and good works. In his view, the Catholic Church had sunk into sinfulness, greed, and loose morals. He believed that popes, cardinals, and bishops often had forgotten their vows of chastity, or sexual purity, and had mistresses and children. Popes had more interest in war than peace, he said. Luther accused church leaders of sleeping in fur-covered beds while the poor slept outdoors. He was shocked that they ate massive meals washed down with the finest wines and filled their homes with more riches than many kings owned.

But Luther could not let his time in Rome pass by without trying to satisfy his own spiritual needs. He wanted to shorten his own time in purgatory as well as his grandfather's, who had died recently. He climbed the Sacred Stairs on his knees. On each of the 28 steps, he said a required prayer. At the top, he wondered, "Who knows whether this is really true?"

Luther and his companion finally left Rome, once again tramping through the snowy Alps, to return to Erfurt. Their mission on behalf of the Observant Augustinians had failed. The leader of the Augustinian order had refused to hear their case. The monks wanted to appeal their case further, but Luther would have nothing to do with it. He decided to obey his superiors. His brothers at the monastery were furious. They said he should go live with von Staupitz in Wittenberg.

For Luther, the next few months at Erfurt were filled with conflicts in the order and a continuing personal spiritual battle over his own salvation. In the summer of 1511, Luther left Erfurt to live at the Black Cloister, the Augustinian monastery in Wittenberg. There he continued to have spiritual battles. He was troubled when he tried to pray and said the devil himself was tormenting him. He told how the tempter provoked him by saying, "Do you think that God hears your prayer and pays any attention?"

Meanwhile, von Staupitz tried to convince Luther that he only needed to love God. But Luther would argue that no one can love an angry, judgmental God who sends souls to the flames of hell. He questioned God, and he questioned whether his best would ever be good enough to satisfy such a holy God.

Von Staupitz was growing tired of Luther's doubts and his six-hour confessions. He ordered him to study for a doctorate, preach at St. Mary's Church in town, and teach at the monastery. "It will be the death of me!" Luther responded to his superior, who was now

When Luther had doubts about his standing before God, von Staupitz helped him.

his closest friend. But keeping Luther busy was von Staupitz' way of getting him out of spiritual despair.

The following year, in 1512, Luther received his doctoral degree in theology from the University of Wittenberg. Elector Frederick paid the required fee for his degree. The customary woolen doctor's cap

In 1512, Luther became a professor at the University of Wittenberg.

was placed on Luther's head, and the traditional silver doctor's ring was placed on his finger. In October 1512, 28-year-old Dr. Martin Luther began lecturing at the University of Wittenberg. He also preached at the Castle Church, taught at the monastery, read Scripture at meals, supervised 11 monasteries, and even managed a fishpond.

For the next five years, in his small room in the tower above the arch in the monastery, he struggled with how he could live in the presence of a just God. He feverishly studied the Bible—Psalms, Romans, Galatians, and Hebrews—to prepare for his university lectures and to find answers to his questions. He began to see God in a different way. He came to believe there was nothing he could do to satisfy God. He turned to a belief that Christ had satisfied God on his behalf by dying on the cross. He wrote:

> *He [Christ] died for me, he made his righteousness mine and made my sin his own; and if he made my sin his own, then I do not have it, and I am free.*

Luther now was convinced that he could only stand before a just God because of grace—God's kindness to an undeserving person. He believed good deeds would then happen naturally. In 1515, Luther began his lectures on a book from the Bible called Romans. He began with these words:

In the presence of God it is not by doing just works that one becomes just, but, having been made just, one does just deeds.

The writings of the Apostle Paul in the Bible were especially meaningful to Luther. One of the passages that held great significance for him was in the New Testament book of Romans:

Therefore we conclude that a man is justified by faith without the deeds of the law.

Luther's new beliefs were contrary to everything he had been taught. They went against the doctrines of the Catholic Church and what nearly every person in the Holy Roman Empire believed. But Luther was satisfied with the answer he had found to his burning question. He later wrote:

All at once I felt that I had been born again and entered into paradise itself through open gates. Immediately I saw the whole of Scripture in a different light.

He began to teach, preach, and talk openly about his new beliefs. Before long, he was attracting standing-room-only crowds for his sermons. He boldly proclaimed that salvation was a gift of God's grace through Christ, received by faith. He also taught that a person could approach God without going

Luther preached at the Castle Church and St. Mary's Church in Wittenberg.

through the church or a priest. Luther's message was very popular.

The church could no longer hold the people who wanted to hear what Luther had to say. But many others would consider his teachings heresy. ❧

Chapter

4 95 TOPICS
OF DEBATE

⤬

In 1517, Luther was lecturing on two books of the Bible—Galatians and Hebrews. While he was teaching about grace, the Catholic Church was increasing its efforts to sell indulgences. Pope Leo wanted to finish a building in Rome called St. Peter's Basilica, but there wasn't enough money. Leo's extravagant lifestyle and financial support of art and culture had nearly depleted church funds. The best way to raise money, the pope declared, was to increase the sale of indulgences. He believed people would be happy to have more opportunities to release themselves or their loved ones from the penalties of sin.

Johann Tetzel, a stumpy Dominican monk, was one of Leo's best salesmen. He went freely from town to town throughout most of Germany selling

On October 31, 1517, Martin Luther nailed his Ninety-Five Theses to the door of the Castle Church in Wittenberg, Germany.

Frederick III (also known as Frederick the Wise) was elector of Saxony and protector of Martin Luther.

indulgences. Frederick the Wise wouldn't allow Tetzel to enter Saxony, however. Frederick had his own collection of religious relics in Wittenberg, and he didn't want competition. But in the rest of Germany, Tetzel's purpose was simple—sell as many passes out of purgatory as possible.

Grand preparations were made for Tetzel's visits. Publicity announced his coming, and stages were built for his performances. Before he entered a town, drummers, trumpeters, and heralds on horses announced his arrival. Then he would ride in on a horse with his armed guard and the pope's coat of arms. On top of a tall cross, raised high so all could see, was an example of what he would offer Catholics that day— an indulgence. Then Tetzel took his place on the platform and began to preach:

> *Do you not hear the voices of your dead relatives and others, crying out to you and saying, "Pity us, pity us, for we are in dire punishment and torment from which*

you can redeem us for a pittance"? And
you will not?

His fiery sermons presented vivid details of the agonies his listeners and their loved ones would suffer for their sins. As a final encouragement to buy indulgences, Tetzel would add:

German priest Johann Tetzel (1465–1519) went from town to town selling indulgences.

Once the coin into the coffer clings, a soul
from purgatory heavenward springs!

Then Tetzel opened for business. On a table was an ample supply of blank indulgences. People flocked to purchase them. Some people, however, criticized Tetzel and the strategies of the church. Luther certainly raised a critical eyebrow at what the church was doing.

That year, Tetzel visited many places, including two towns just 20 miles (32 km) from Wittenberg. When some people returned to Wittenberg with their indulgences, Luther reacted. On October 31, 1517, he nailed a large piece of paper called a broadsheet to the door of the Castle Church. He called it *Disputation on the Power and Efficacy of Indulgences.*

In his own handwriting in Latin, Luther invited students and professors to a debate. He began with these words:

> *Out of love and zeal for truth and the desire to bring it to light, the following theses will be publicly discussed at Wittenberg under the chairmanship of the reverend father Martin Luther, Master of Arts and Sacred Theology and regularly appointed Lecturer on these subjects at that place. He requests that those who cannot be present to debate orally with us will do so by letter.*

There were 95 topics of discussion. He wanted to discuss penance, confession, guilt, humility, purgatory, hell, and heaven. Also on his list were love, salvation, and, of course, indulgences.

Number 52 said:

> It is vain [useless] to trust in salvation
> by indulgence letters, even though the

indulgence commissary [distributor], or even the pope, were to offer his soul as security.

He also wondered why the pope didn't just empty purgatory. After all, if he had the power to set some free, then why not let them all out? Luther's 82nd topic of debate read:

Why does not the pope empty purgatory for the sake of holy love and the dire need of the souls that are there if he redeems an infinite number of souls for the sake of miserable money with which to build a church?

Leo X (1475–1521) served as pope of the Catholic Church from 1513 until his death in 1521.

Luther also suggested that the pope would do better to sell St. Peter's Basilica and give the money to the poor. Luther sent a copy of his topics to Archbishop Albrecht, the religious leader of three large territories. He included a letter that condemned the sale of indulgences.

Albrecht was shocked by Luther's 95 topics of

discussion. "God on High!" he said. "Is this how souls entrusted to your care are taught?" Albrecht sent a copy of the list to Pope Leo X. At first, the pope thought Luther's words were nothing more than a monkish quarrel. But what came to be called Luther's *Ninety-Five Theses* was about to cause an uproar throughout Europe.

Luther had intended to spark an academic discussion, but he could not control what happened next. Someone translated the list into German and had thousands of copies printed and circulated. Tetzel's large crowds diminished, and critics jeered at him. Sales of indulgences slowed down and much less money came in.

Later Luther would say, "I would never have thought that such a storm would rise from Rome over one simple scrap of paper."

Pope Leo X largely ignored Martin Luther. Leo was more interested in hunting, planning attacks on Jerusalem, and supporting the arts. He wanted Rome to be the cultural center of Europe. While he was head of the Catholic Church, he supported artists, poets, architects, musicians, and others who came to Rome to make it a magnificent city. Among them were famous artists Michelangelo and Raphael.

5 CHARGED WITH HERESY

❦

During the winter of 1517 to 1518, Luther went about teaching and preaching as usual. He finished his lectures on Galatians and Hebrews, still emphasizing salvation by grace through faith. He hoped his ideas would spread throughout the university. He also worked to find a professor who could teach Greek and Hebrew, the original languages in which the Bible was written. He wanted to be able to study the original words of the Scriptures.

More and more people were embracing Luther's ideas. But as his friends and followers increased, so did his enemies. Johann Eck, a priest and professor at the University of Ingolstadt, became one of his strongest foes. Previously his friend, Eck now accused Luther of heresy. Tetzel and his fellow Dominicans

At Leipzig, Germany, Martin Luther (right) and Johann Eck debated for 23 days. The University of Leipzig declared Eck the winner.

51 ∽

were also determined to prove that Luther was wrong and guilty of heresy.

In the spring of 1518, Luther was invited to Heidelberg for a gathering of the Augustinians. He was asked to defend his stand on indulgences. Because he had so many enemies, he needed protection. Frederick the Wise thought highly of Luther and provided him with a letter assuring his safety during travel.

An indulgence had a blank area where the purchaser could fill in a name of the person whose time in purgatory would be shortened.

He arrived safely at Heidelberg and presented the Augustinian order with 28 topics of discussion. None of them mentioned indulgences. But he took the opportunity to clearly explain his new beliefs. He

boldly proclaimed:

> *The law says, "Do this!" and it is never done. Grace says, "Believe in this man [Christ]!" and immediately everything is done.*

Meanwhile, in Rome, Pope Leo gave his religious adviser, Sylvester Prierias, the task of examining Luther's *Ninety-Five Theses*. Prierias, an older priest and a Dominican, quickly declared that Luther was wrong. He wrote the *Dialogus*, his official claim against Luther, and sent it to the pope's lawyers. They drew up a formal charge against Luther.

The job of sending the *Dialogus* and the formal charge to Luther was given to Thomas Cajetan. He was head of the Dominicans and a cardinal, second in power just below the pope. Luther received the documents on August 7, 1518. He was ordered to appear in Rome to answer charges of heresy.

Luther was hesitant to go to Rome. The penalty for condemned heretics was usually torture

The Franciscans and Dominicans are religious orders of the Roman Catholic Church. Members of an order live apart from society to dedicate themselves to religious principles. Some orders are totally isolated (cloistered) from the outside world. Others participate in society by teaching or serving the sick and poor. The Franciscans follow the teachings of St. Francis, who lived a life of hard work and service. The Dominicans follow St. Dominic, who devoted his life to preaching.

followed by burning at the stake. Luther had 60 days to answer the charges. The next day, he wrote a letter to an old friend, George Spalatin, who was now Frederick's personal secretary. He begged Spalatin to persuade Frederick and the emperor to transfer his case to Germany.

In the meantime, the pope changed the order—Luther could meet with Cardinal Cajetan in Augsburg. Cajetan was going there anyway as the pope's representative at an Imperial Diet, a meeting of the leaders of the empire. The pope said that if Luther did not recant his statements against the church, Cajetan could put Luther in chains and take him to Rome. The pope also sent a letter to Frederick—urging him to cooperate with Cajetan.

In September, Frederick ordered Luther to go to Augsburg. Luther obeyed, but not without hesitation and great fear that he might not return alive. Cajetan had been ordered not to debate with Luther. He was to get Luther to say one word—*revoco*—I recant.

Luther and Cajetan met at a private home. With Luther were von Staupitz and a lawyer. Luther had been instructed on how to act in the presence of a cardinal. When he came into Cajetan's presence, he fell flat on his face and said nothing. When Cajetan spoke, Luther rose to his knees.

Not until Cajetan told him to do so did Luther stand up. Then the cardinal ordered him to do three

things: first, repent of his errors and recant; second, promise not to teach them again; and third, do not disturb the peace of the church.

Although Luther was only supposed to say *revoco*, he dared to ask Cajetan what his errors were. When Cajetan explained, Luther replied that he could not

Martin Luther defended his beliefs before Cardinal Thomas Cajetan in Augsburg, Germany, in 1518.

recant. Cajetan said, "You must recant this today, no matter what you wish." But Luther would not.

The two men met again the next day and talked about the authority of the pope and his right to grant indulgences. Then Luther asked if he could reply in writing. A third meeting was scheduled. When Luther came before Cajetan the third time, he brought with him what he had written. Cajetan was polite and promised to send the document to Rome but then reminded Luther that it was now time to recant. The argument became heated, and Cajetan exploded. "Go now, and do not appear before me again until you are ready to recant!" Luther left the room. He later wrote to a friend:

> *I would be the most accommodating and beloved person if I were to say the simple word revoco, that is, "I recant." But I will not become a heretic by denying the understanding through which I have been made a Christian.*

Luther now realized he was in trouble. Secretly, von Staupitz released him from his vows, so he was free to flee. Then von Staupitz and Luther's lawyer sneaked out of the city after dark. On the night of October 20, 1518, Luther fled on an old horse through a hole in the city's wall and headed to Wittenberg. He arrived on October 31, exactly one year after he had

posted his *Ninety-Five Theses* on the church door. Now he could only fear and hope. He was in Saxony, however, and under the protection of Frederick.

Over the next several weeks, a flurry of letters and decrees were exchanged. A letter Luther wrote to Frederick convinced the elector that he was doing the right thing by protecting him. Then Frederick wrote to Cajetan and told him he would not send Luther to Rome until he was convicted of heresy.

On December 13, 1518, Pope Leo published a new decree. He confirmed he had the right to issue indulgences and that they were a good way to do

Luther refused to recant when he met with Cajetan. On October 20, 1518, he fled Augsburg and headed to Wittenberg.

penance. The decree didn't name Luther in particular, but it condemned all monks and preachers who taught to the contrary.

Luther expected that Rome would condemn him soon. But he went back to teaching at the university. In January 1519, Frederick summoned Luther to his residence to meet with a special representative of the pope. Luther was asked to recant, but again he refused. However, Luther agreed to be silent if his opponents would also be silent.

That same month, Maximilian I, emperor of the Holy Roman Empire, died. Pope Leo now put his energies into supporting Frederick the Wise as candidate for the next emperor. He didn't want Charles I, Maximilian's grandson, to be elected, since that would give him too much power. Leo virtually ignored Luther during this time.

In June, some of the pope's attention turned to Luther. A debate was planned between Luther and Johann Eck, who would serve as the pope's representative. It would take place in the city of Leipzig.

The large procession that traveled with Luther from Wittenberg to Leipzig included his closest followers and about 200 university students. The debate was an impressive event that began with Mass and a large formal meal.

An important event also took place on the first

day of the debate. A new emperor was elected—
Maximilian's grandson, Charles I of Spain—as Leo
had feared. Now he was called Emperor Charles V.

But the people of Leipzig were more interested
in the Luther-Eck debate. Sixty-five armed guards
protected the debaters, and 200 students roamed the
town. Luther's supporters were there, but so were
Eck's. The debate lasted 23 days. Eck, a gifted, clever
debater with a powerful speaking voice, pushed
Luther to admit that he denied the authority of the
pope. Luther declared that Christ, not the pope, was

Charles V was emperor of the Holy Roman Empire from 1519 to 1556, when he resigned his position and retired to a monastery in Spain.

the head of the church.

When the debate ended, Luther was certain he'd lost. Eck sent him a letter accusing him of being the worst of all heretics. Luther declared that Eck was shameless. Luther had made some enemies and lost a few friends, but he also had acquired many followers. The debate made him a well-known man. His books began selling by the thousands. The number of students at Wittenberg University grew rapidly. Luther's classes overflowed with up to 400 students. His church couldn't hold the number of people who wanted to hear his sermons.

In February 1520, a commission met in Rome to determine whether Luther's writings contained heresy. His situation was becoming dangerous. Two German noblemen offered him their assistance and protection. A few months later, someone offered 100 knights to protect him wherever he went.

In Rome, on June 24, 1520, Pope Leo issued a papal bull, an official decree signed by the pope. The *Exsurge Domine (Arise, Lord)*, as it was called, gave Luther 60 days to recant or be excommunicated— barred from Mass or from receiving the sacraments of the church.

The pope also ordered that Luther's books be burned in public. In response, Luther built a fire under a large oak tree in Wittenberg and publicly burned the *Exsurge Domine* and the entire canon, or

laws, of the Catholic Church.

People continued to buy Luther's books. His *Address to the Christian Nobility of the German Nation*, sold out in two weeks. In it, Luther attacked the idea that priests were more important than common people. Priests had no special authority over Christians, he claimed. All believers were priests, he said, and could come directly to God.

In October, his new book, *On the Babylonian Captivity of the Church*, declared that priests held

Luther publicly burned the papal bull in which the pope ordered him to take back 41 of his 95 theses within 60 days.

people captive through sacraments and good works. Luther compared the pope to the Antichrist himself and said the necessary sacraments should be reduced from seven to two—baptism and the Lord's Supper.

Frederick was being pressured to burn Luther's books, arrest him, and send him to Rome. But Frederick refused and insisted that Luther should receive a hearing in Saxony before impartial judges.

In the meantime, Emperor Charles V scheduled an Imperial Diet in the city of Worms for early 1521. The purpose of the diet was to allow Charles to establish his authority over the German princes and unite these leaders, who seldom agreed. He also wanted to

With his left hand, Luther points to the pope, monks, and cardinals, who, he believed, were corrupt. His right hand points to Christ. Before him, the bread and wine of communion are being served to worshipers, which went against the teachings of the Catholic Church at that time.

discuss the threat of armies outside the empire.

At Frederick's request, Charles allowed Luther to appear. Girolama Aleander, a cardinal and the pope's ambassador to the diet, objected. He insisted that Charles do his duty and declare Luther an outlaw.

On January 3, 1521, the pope issued another bull, *Decet Romanum Pontificem*, excommunicating Luther. It was sent to Charles with instructions to announce it at the diet and declare that any territory or church that protected Luther would be banned from the empire.

The diet opened on January 28. Cardinal Aleander persuaded Charles to allow him to issue an imperial edict against Luther. However, on February 19, the princes warned Charles that condemning Luther without a hearing might cause a revolution. Charles agreed and allowed Luther to appear at the diet. He could travel under safe passage—no one could seize or arrest him for any reason. ❧

6 THE DIET OF WORMS

ᏋᏒᎧᏒᎧ

In April 1521, Luther and his small party of companions set out for Worms. They traveled through Erfurt, where he preached at the Augustinian monastery to a crowd that overflowed into the courtyard. From city to city, crowds greeted him with cheers. His popularity grew at each stop.

On April 16, an imperial herald led Luther into Worms as trumpeters announced his arrival. About 2,000 people gathered to usher him through the city gates. Aleander described Luther's popularity:

> Nine-tenths of the Germans shout "Long Live Luther," and the other tenth, "Death to Rome."

Luther was met with cheering crowds as he traveled to Worms to attend the Imperial Diet.

Worms was a city in celebration. A diet brought wealthy princes and bishops to a city. Along the streets, jugglers and jesters entertained. Vendors set up tables to sell food and drink. But Luther was not there to join in the festivities. He was there to defend his beliefs. Before he left Wittenberg, he had declared that he was not going to Worms to recant. He wanted to debate. He was not afraid this time, as he had been at Augsburg. He stated with confidence:

> *Unless I am held back by force, or Caesar [Charles V] takes back his invitation, I will enter Worms under the banner of Christ against the gates of hell.*

On April 17, two officials of the Roman Empire led Luther secretly to the diet in order to avoid the crowds. At about 4 P.M., Luther entered the room. Before him were the ruler of the most powerful empire in the world and the top Catholic representatives from Rome. Throughout the room were soldiers and the most politically powerful men of Germany.

In the middle of the room was a table piled high with books written by Martin Luther, son of a miner, simple monk of the Augustinian order, and small-town priest and professor. Luther stood next to the table. The person who was appointed to question Luther pointed to the books and asked him two questions. Had he written these books? Did he defend them all,

or did he now choose to recant part of them?

Luther now realized there would be no debate or hearing. He answered in a very soft voice. The books, indeed, were his, and he had written more. But he asked for more time to answer the second question. After all, it had to do with the salvation of souls. The emperor gave him one day.

Back at his quarters, Luther wrote:

> *So long as Christ is merciful, I will not recant a single jot or tittle [tiniest bit].*

Luther defended his antichurch writings before Holy Roman Emperor Charles V at the Diet of Worms in 1521.

Luther's appearance before the diet the next day was delayed until 6 P.M. In the candlelight, he was again asked whether he would recant some of what he had written. Luther began to give a short speech, but the examiner would have nothing to do with it. He declared that Luther must give a simple answer.

Luther answered that he could not and would not retract. He added, "May God help me. Amen."

The room exploded in shouts and excitement. Charles walked out. Some heard Luther shout, "I am finished!" and saw him make a gesture of victory. Luther had calmly defended his beliefs and, in doing so, had condemned what the Catholic Church had taught for a thousand years.

Aleander set to writing a document, called the Edict of Worms, that would make Luther an unprotected outlaw. Charles would not sign it yet, however. He first fulfilled his promise to give Luther safe passage.

Luther left Worms as a protected man. Along the way, he attracted huge crowds and spoke in monasteries and churches. At

In politics, a diet is a formal meeting of the leaders of an empire or country. The word diet comes from the Latin word dies, which means day. The word came to be used in this way because the meetings took place on a daily basis and usually lasted for several months. Some of the most famous diets of the Holy Roman Empire were the Diet of Worms (January 28 through May 26, 1521), the Diets of Nuremberg (1522, 1524, 1532), and the Diet of Augsburg (1530).

The map shows:

ICELAND

The Vatican
Rome
Papal Gardens
Sistine Chapel (completed in 1483)
St. Peter's Square (completed in 1667)
Basilica of St. Peter (completed in 1626)
wall

Holy Roman Empire, 1500
Map shows present-day boundaries.

FINLAND
NORWAY
SWEDEN
ESTONIA RUSSIA
LATVIA
LITH.
RUS.
BELARUS
North Sea
DENMARK
Baltic Sea
IRELAND
UNITED KINGDOM
London
NETH. Wittenberg POLAND
BEL. GERMANY
ATLANTIC OCEAN
CZECH REP. UKRAINE
Worms
LUX.
Basel SLOVAKIA
0   300 miles
0   300 kilometers
FRANCE SWITZ. AUSTRIA HUNGARY
SLOV. ROMANIA
CRO.
ITALY BOS. & HERZ. SERB. & MONT. BULGARIA
Adriatic Sea
The Vatican (see inset)
Rome MAC.
ALB.
PORTUGAL SPAIN
GREECE
Mediterranean Sea
N E S W

Möhra, he visited relatives and preached to a group of peasants outdoors. The town didn't have a church.

Luther left Möhra in May but didn't make it back to Wittenberg. Someone had other plans for him. ☙

The Protestant Reformation began in Germany, but it affected all of Europe and eventually the whole world.

Chapter

7 JUNKER JÖRG

❧

On the afternoon of May 4, 1521, Luther and three others set out from Möhra in a horse-drawn wagon. As they passed through the Thuringian forest in the dark, four armed and hooded horsemen charged out of the woods and demanded to know which one was Luther. The driver pointed to Luther, and the men seized him and dragged him up the road.

Many thought they would never see Luther again. But the kidnapping had been staged by Frederick the Wise. The plan was to take him to the Wartburg Castle near Eisenach, where he would be safe. A little before midnight, a blindfolded Luther was taken across the drawbridge and deposited at a castle owned by Frederick and inhabited by his knights.

So he wouldn't be recognized, Luther exchanged

Disguised as a knight, Luther lived in the Wartburg Castle for about 10 months.

his monk's cowel, or hooded black robe, for the clothes of a knight. Hidden in a room with a retractable staircase, Luther let his hair and beard grow and called himself Junker Jörg (Knight George).

Living at the castle was not a pleasant experience for Luther, who was used to a busy schedule of teaching, preaching, writing, studying, and traveling. Sometimes, he became depressed and suffered from an upset stomach. He wrote to his friend and fellow professor, Philipp Melanchthon:

Luther was often depressed and ill at the Wartburg Castle. During his stay, he translated the entire New Testament portion of the Bible into German.

> *I sit here like a fool and, hardened in leisure, pray little, do not sigh for the Church of God.*

Before long, Luther began reading the Bible daily. He had managed to grab his Hebrew Old Testament and Greek New Testament when he was kidnapped. He also started writing. Over the next 10 months, he wrote and published 12 books and translated the New Testament into German. The New Testament went on sale in 1522, and more than 5,000 copies were sold in the first two months. Over the next 24 years, nearly 300,000 copies would be sold.

Johannes Gutenberg's (c. 1398-1468) development of the printing press in the 1450s played an important role in the Protestant Reformation. Because books and pamphlets could be printed and distributed by the thousands, Luther's ideas spread quickly throughout Europe.

On May 26, 1521, Charles V signed the Edict of Worms in front of the few who still remained at the Diet of Worms. It made Luther an official outlaw of the Holy Roman Empire. Anyone could seize him and kill him, and citizens were obligated to turn him in.

Some people reacted strongly to his radical ideas. Three European universities openly condemned his teachings. Professors of religion wrote against his doctrines. But in Wittenberg, the fires of reformation were burning strong. With Luther gone, leadership fell to three of Luther's friends: Philipp Melanchthon, Andreas Karlstadt, and Gabriel Zwilling. Under their direction, people were drastically changing the way they believed and worshipped. Priests weren't celebrating Mass and administering communion according to Catholic tradition. Three priests, one of them Karlstadt, broke their vows of celibacy and got married. Thirteen monks left the Augustinian monastery. On November 1, 1521, at the Castle Church, Luther's friend and fellow professor, Justus Jonas, declared that indulgences were rubbish.

Students turned to rioting and attacking churches. They took Mass books from the altars, drove out priests, and hurled rocks at worshipers. Knife-wielding protesters ruined holy statues and destroyed an altar at a Franciscan monastery. They rioted in the streets and broke church windows. Wittenberg's town council was afraid that a full-scale revolution would soon break out.

Luther got word of the turmoil. In early December, he stole out of the Wartburg Castle on horseback, in full disguise as a knight, and headed for Wittenberg. No one recognized him the entire week he was there. He freely observed what was going on—and he was shocked. He rode back to the castle and furiously wrote *Admonition to All True Christians to Guard Themselves Against Sedition.* In it, he proclaimed there were never any grounds for riot or rebellion.

On Christmas Day, 1521, about 2,000 people, nearly the whole town of Wittenberg, assembled at the Castle Church. Karlstadt put aside his priestly robes and began celebrating Mass. He started in

Latin but then changed to German. For the first time, the people heard Mass in their own language. Then he shared communion with the people. Until then, only the bread had been shared with the people. Now Karlstadt also served them the wine. His acts went against the very laws of the Catholic Church.

Luther secretly left the Wartburg Castle on December 1521 to find out why university students were rioting in Wittenberg.

At Karlstadt's urging, the Wittenberg town council issued the first city law concerning church reform. Mass was to be conducted as Karlstadt had done, and statues were to be removed from churches. The council also looked to Luther for leadership and invited him to return. Luther notified Frederick that he was coming back to Wittenberg. Although he was still under the ban of the Edict of Worms, he returned on March 6, 1522, to try to calm the storm. Since his arrest probably would have caused huge riots, authorities left him alone.

On March 9, Luther again took his place behind the pulpit at St. Mary's Church. For eight days, he preached about patience, love, and consideration for the weak. The violence that had gone on was

Since Luther's time, the doors of the Castle Church have been replaced with bronze doors engraved with the Ninety-Five Theses.

horrifying to him, and he told the people he could not defend their actions. He was ashamed to have fighting, threats, and destruction connected to his teachings and his name. He even said he was ready to leave Wittenberg forever.

But he continued to preach passionately, trying to fix what had happened while he had been at the Wartburg Castle. Gradually, Luther formed a group of faithful followers who understood what he believed, a doctrine that came to be known as the Wittenberg Theology.

Luther's followers were known as Protestants, Lutherans, or sometimes Martinians. The Protestant movement spread rapidly throughout Europe. In Switzerland, Ulrich Zwingli and John Calvin sought to reform the Catholic Church. In Strasbourg, Martin Bucer taught Protestant beliefs. Large crowds were soon embracing Luther's beliefs.

The Castle Church, where Martin Luther nailed his Ninety-Five Theses to the door, still stands in Wittenberg, Germany. In 1760, during the Seven Years' War (1756–1763), it was seriously damaged by fire. It was restored and portions rebuilt in the late 1800s. The badly burned wooden doors were replaced. St. Mary's Church, where Luther often preached, and the Augustinian monastery where he lived are also still there. The town is now officially cailed Lutherstadt Wittenberg.

Others turned against Luther when they didn't agree with him on certain issues. Karlstadt left Wittenberg and ended up opposing him. Some, like Thomas Müntzer, one of Luther's earlier

Thomas Müntzer, a German pastor, was the rebel leader of the peasants who rose up against their masters in 1524 and 1525.

followers, believed the wicked should be destroyed and Catholic churches burned. Luther called them *Schwärmgeister*, or spirits who swarm about like mad bees.

Luther's ideas even spread beyond the church. The German economy depended on peasants, who worked for very little, while their masters grew rich. In 1524, German peasants banded together against their masters. Their champion was Martin Luther, who had once warned the nobles that people neither could nor would endure their tyranny any longer. He added that even God would not endure it.

Luther had hoped to bring equality and peace. Instead, a full-scale war broke out with Müntzer as the leader. In spring of 1525, about 300,000 peasants destroyed crops and hundreds of churches, monasteries, and castles. Luther traveled from town to town, urging them to act peacefully.

Because Luther spoke out against their violence, most peasants now considered him their enemy and even threatened him. Luther returned to Wittenberg,

On April 16, 1525, during the Peasants' War, a group of peasants killed a nobleman named Count von Helfenstein, as his wife watched.

angry at the senseless destruction. In May, he wrote *Against the Murderous and Thieving Hordes of Peasants.* He encouraged princes to slay the peasants if they didn't lay down their arms. Even as he wrote, the princes were doing just that. Peasants were seized and executed by the thousands in what came to be called the Peasants' War.

As the war came to a violent end, Luther sometimes regretted what had become of his simple message. He now turned to his personal life. He would soon do what many of his fellow priests and monks had already done—get married. ॐ

Chapter
8 KATHARINA VON BORA

ꜱꜱꜱ

It had been a little over two years since a group of 12 Catholic nuns had embraced Luther's beliefs through reading his books. They rejected their religious vows and asked to leave their convent. The Catholic Church denied their request. But in April 1523, they escaped and showed up in Wittenberg as Protestants and followers of Luther.

Some of the young nuns returned to their families. Others stayed in Wittenberg, where Luther found husbands for many of them. One nun in particular— Katharina von Bora—had refused all of Luther's suggestions for husbands. The story goes that she would only agree to marry Luther himself.

On June 13, 1525, 41-year-old Martin Luther married 26-year-old Katie, as he called her.

Katharina von Bora (1499–1552), ex-nun and wife of Martin Luther

Luther wrote:

> *Suddenly, unexpectedly, and while my mind was on other matters, the Lord has snared me with the yoke of marriage.*

Katharina von Bora and Martin Luther were married on June 13, 1525, at a private home in Wittenberg.

It was a simple wedding. Among the guests were Luther's parents, delighted that their son was getting married. The marriage raised eyebrows across Europe, however. Catholic leaders were against it, of course, but even some Protestants believed Luther

should dedicate himself to church reform, not personal comforts.

Martin and Katie's first home was the Black Cloister, which no longer operated as a monastery. It was a wedding gift from John Frederick, the new elector of Saxony. Luther's longtime protector, Frederick the Wise, died a month before the wedding. Now his brother John was in charge.

Katie managed their large home with good organization and hard work. She washed clothes, changed linens, raised and sold cattle, managed the brewery, and tended the garden and orchard. She also stocked the fishpond and raised chickens. When the Luthers needed meat, Katie did the butchering. Martin helped out, but most of his time was spent speaking, writing, and teaching.

There was a steady stream of students and other visitors at the Luthers' home. There were often 30 or more guests at a time, all of them wanting to talk to the master reformer himself. Visitors had to be fed, their rooms cleaned, and their laundry done. When they were sick, Katie and Martin cared for them and even brewed herbal remedies to treat their illnesses. The cost of tending to visitors, along with Martin's

> *When Katharina von Bora was quite young, her mother died. Her father remarried and sent 5-year-old Katharina to a convent. Her Aunt Magadalene was a nun there, and her Aunt Margarete was the Mother Superior in charge of the convent. In 1515, at the age of 16, Katharina took her vows to become a nun.*

generous gifts to them, became a major drain on their income. They often had little money left over.

Martin enjoyed married life. He wrote, "There is a lot to get used to in the first year of marriage. One wakes up in the morning and finds a pair of pigtails on the pillow which were not there before." Yet he approved of marriage, saying, "There is no bond on earth so sweet, nor any separation so bitter, as that which occurs in a good marriage."

Within a year, the first of the Luthers' six children arrived. Martin and Katie named their son Hans, after Martin's father. Three girls and two more boys followed in the next eight years, and they would

Katharina and Martin Luther with five of their children. In the background is their friend, Philipp Melanchthon.

adopt four more besides.

Luther often suffered from health problems. He had ringing in his ears, heart trouble, and nearly constant indigestion. His ailments often caused him to be depressed and to suffer mental and spiritual battles. During those times, he often composed music; many have become well-known hymns of the Christian faith, such as "A Mighty Fortress Is Our God." Part of the lyrics declared:

> *A mighty fortress is our God,*
> *A bulwark never failing.*
> *Our helper He amid the flood*
> *Of mortal ills prevailing.*

Summer of 1527 brought the Black Plague to Wittenberg. While many fled the city, Luther stayed, tirelessly caring for the sick. Katie was pregnant that year and in December gave birth to a daughter, Elizabeth. The baby was sickly and lived only a few months. Luther's heart was broken.

Although his mind had been on family and health that year, Luther's religious reforms continued to spread rapidly throughout Europe. Conflicts were also growing. In 1530, Charles V summoned the elector of Saxony and the princes to another Imperial Diet in Augsburg. A group of six princes wanted to present the Lutheran beliefs at the diet. Melanchthon was called upon to write a clear statement of the

Lutheran faith and explain how it was different from the beliefs of the Catholic Church. On April 3, Luther and some of his followers accompanied the elector on his journey to Augsburg. Luther, however, was left at Coburg Castle, about 100 miles (160 km) from Augsburg. Since he was still an outlaw and could be arrested, he couldn't attend the diet.

The Diet of Augsburg dragged on into the summer. Finally, on June 25, the statement of faith, called the *Augsburg Confession*, was presented to the emperor. The six princes had it read aloud in German and Latin to Charles and the other princes. When Luther heard that his confession of faith had been read to all the leaders of Germany, he rejoiced:

> *I am tremendously pleased to have lived to this moment when Christ has been publicly proclaimed by his staunch confessors in such a great assembly by means of this truly most beautiful confession!*

The church's response—*Confutation of the Augsburg Confession*, written by Johann Eck—was immediate and heated. Eck demanded that Charles and other leaders submit to the *Confutation*. One prince who supported Luther left the diet in protest. Others discussed an alliance.

In August, the controversy was still being debated. Luther was concerned about how this was going to

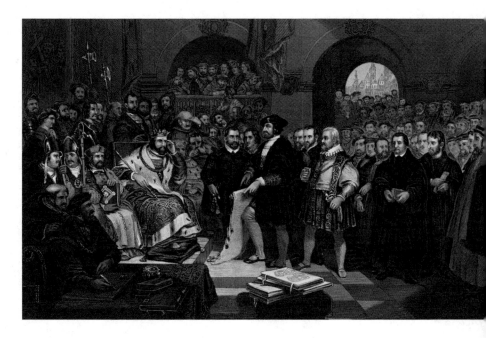

affect Germany. He was afraid a war might come out of this, but there was nothing he could do. In the end, the Roman emperor rejected the *Augsburg Confession.* Luther was disappointed and proclaimed that the Catholic Church and those who defended it were hopelessly wrong. He told Christians to no longer even pray for the pope.

Philipp Melanchthon wrote the Augsburg Confession that was presented to Emperor Charles V at the Diet of Augsburg in 1530.

Forty-six-year-old Luther, still suffering from bad health, relentlessly continued to preach and teach. Spreading his religious ideas and debating those who disagreed with him filled much of his life. He was the heart and the center of the Reformation. He could not give in to illness when so many people still needed to be taught what he believed to be the truth. ✑

9 ALTERING THE COURSE OF HISTORY

ⱾⱯⱯⱯⱯⱯ

As Luther grew older, he focused on educating the next generation. He wrote the *Small Catechism* and *Large Catechism*, religious training manuals for children and young pastors and teachers.

He also continued to debate those who opposed him. He had already spent years arguing with Desiderius Erasmus, a Catholic scholar and writer. Erasmus had urged the Catholic Church to change but did not break away from it, as Luther and his followers did. The two men disagreed fiercely, attacking each other in published works. But Erasmus recognized how popular Luther was and eventually compared their debates to a "fly taking on an elephant."

In 1540, when Luther was 56 years old, an old man for that time, the issue of marriage came up again.

A fellow reformer had asked Luther to support his desire to marry a second wife. Bigamy, or marriage to more than one spouse, was against the law. When Luther didn't condemn the marriage, he caused quite a stir among Catholics and Protestants alike. He only stated that divorce was a greater problem than bigamy. People would endlessly criticize him for that statement and for some of his later writings about Muslim and Jewish people.

In 1542, Luther's 13-year-old daughter Magdalena died. It was a very painful time for him and Katie. In addition, he was distressed by what was happening in Wittenberg. The enthusiasm of the reform movement had dulled, and worldly interests had become more important to many. Luther described the town as immoral and wrote, "My heart has become cold, so that I do not like to be there anymore." He spoke out against thieves and murderers and attacked those who he believed were serving the devil. But he was also hopeful for his church. He told Katie:

> *I do not leave behind a sad face of our congregations: they flourish in pure and sound teaching, and they grow day by day through many excellent and sincere pastors.*

In 1545, he journeyed twice to Eisleben, the place of his birth, to help settle a political issue. He went

Present-day Germany
Map shows boundaries of 1500.

DENMARK

Baltic Sea

North Sea

POLAND-LITHUANIA

•Berlin

Magdeburg•

•Wittenberg

Mansfeld•
Eisleben•
•Leipzig

Eisenach•
Wartburg• •Erfurt
Castle
Saxony

H O L Y   R O M A N   E M P I R E

Worms•

•Nuremburg

Speyer•

FRANCE

•Augsburg

•Munich

Lake Constance

0   90 miles
0   90 kilometers

Lake Geneva

VENICE

again in January 1546, but this time he didn't return.

The issue being discussed was settled on February 17, but sometime after 8 P.M., the 62-year-old Luther got pains in his chest. He went to his bed and prayed the common prayer of the dying:

Into your hand I commit my spirit; you have redeemed me, O Lord, faithful God.

Martin Luther was born in Eisleben, Germany, but spent most of his life in Wittenberg.

91

His longtime friend Justus Jonas was at his bedside. At about 3 A.M. on February 18, 1546, Jonas shouted:

Reverend father, are you ready to die trusting in your Lord Jesus Christ?

Luther responded with a firm *Ja!* (Yes!) and died.

Luther's body was brought that day to St. Andrew's church in Eisleben, where Jonas preached a sermon. On February 20, his body, clothed in a long, white robe, was put onto a horse-drawn hearse.

The sermon at Luther's funeral was preached by Johannes Bugenhagen, a pastor and professor at Wittenberg. In his sermon, he said, "God has taken away from us this great teacher, prophet, and divinely sent reformer of the church. Oh, how can we cease mourning and crying?" After the funeral, Bugenhagen took care of Luther's wife and children.

With 65 horsemen and two knights alongside, a large group of mourners began the 75-mile (120-km) trek to Wittenberg. Bells rang out as they passed through German towns.

At Wittenberg's gate stood Katie and her children. There were also pastors, professors, students, city council members, and a huge crowd of other Wittenbergers. The growing crowd made its way to the Castle Church, where Luther had proclaimed what he passionately believed. The church could not hold all who attended the funeral of this man who had changed Wittenberg and the Holy Roman Empire forever.

As was common practice, Luther's body was buried inside the Castle Church, underneath the floor in front of the pulpit. The man who had plunged established religion into reform was dead. But his ideas were still very much alive.

Religious reform continued to engulf Europe like

Martin Luther's tomb inside the Castle Church in Wittenberg, Germany

an avalanche. Protestant churches popped up everywhere. Reformers established their beliefs in England, France, Scotland, Switzerland, and other countries. Today the largest Lutheran populations are in Germany (25.8 million), the United States (13.6 million), Sweden (7.2 million), and Denmark (4.6 million).

The Catholic Church tried to suppress the sweeping reform movement. Those found guilty of heresy were sentenced to death by hanging, burning, or drowning. The church also created the *Index Librorum Prohibitorum (List of Prohibited Books)*, naming all banned books. Of course, it included all of Luther's books and other Protestant writings, but it also listed books about art, literature, and science.

The rise of Luther's ideas brought about social change. Nobles held less power, and conditions for peasants improved. But the Reformation also ushered in bitter religious wars between Protestants and Catholics that would go on for hundreds of years. A century after Luther nailed his *Ninety-Five Theses* to the door of the Castle Church, the Thirty Years' War began. This Catholic versus Protestant war destroyed much of Germany and killed about one-third of the country's population.

The Reformation shook the world and opened a whole new way of looking at religion. It divided the Catholic Church forever. But it gave Catholic leaders the drive to change their church from within in what

A copy of Luther's German translation of the Bible with his handwritten notes in the margins

came to be known as the Counter-Reformation. Eventually, communion was given to worshipers, Bibles were allowed in languages other than Latin, and much later, Mass was celebrated in the language of the people.

Martin Luther was passionate about what he believed, and he fearlessly shared it with everyone—from peasants to princes and emperors. By doing so, he changed religion and the world forever, and altered the course of history. Katharina von Bora Luther fittingly wrote:

> *For who would not be sad and afflicted at the loss of such a precious man as my dear lord was. He did great things not just for a city or a single land, but for the whole world.*

LUTHER'S LIFE

1483

Born at Eisleben,
Germany,
November 10

1501-1505

Attends the
University of Erfurt;
receives bachelor's
and master's degrees

1505

Enters an Augustinian
monastery and
becomes a monk

1500

1497

Vasco da Gama
becomes the first
western European
to find a sea route
to India

1503

Italian artist Leonardo
da Vinci begins paint-
ind the *Mona Lisa*

WORLD EVENTS

1507

Ordained a priest in
the Catholic Church

1508

Lectures one term
at the University of
Wittenberg

1510

Visits Rome,
Italy

1508

Michelangelo
begins painting
the ceiling of the
Sistine Chapel in
Rome, Italy

1509

Henry, Prince of
Wales, at age 18,
becomes King Henry
VIII of England

Life and Times

1517

Posts his *Ninety-Five Theses* to the door of the Castle Church in Wittenberg

1512

Receives a doctoral degree in theology from the University of Wittenberg

1511

Moves to the Black Cloister in Wittenberg, Germany

1515

1517

The first Spanish conquistadors, under Francisco Hernandez de Cordoba, reach the Yucatan Peninsula

1511

Diego Velázquez and Hernán Cortés conquer Cuba

1513

Vasco Nuñez de Balboa is the first European to reach the Pacific Ocean

1518

Meets with Cardinal
Thomas Cajetan in
Augsburg, Germany

1519

Debates Johann Eck
in Leipzig, Germany

1520

Receives the *Exsurge
Domine,* a papal bull
giving him 60 days to
recant

1520

1519

Ferdinand
Magellan leaves
Europe to sail
around the world

1520

Charles V is
crowned emperor
of the Holy Roman
Empire

LUTHER'S LIFE

1521

Excommunicated from
the Catholic Church;
attends the Diet of
Worms; taken to Wartburg
Castle; translates New
Testament into German

1524-1525

Condemns the
Peasants' War

1525

Marries Katharina
von Bora

1524

James V becomes
king of Scotland

1521

War breaks out
between Emperor
Charles V and the
king of France

WORLD EVENTS

1530

Helps create the *Augsburg Confession*

1534

His translation of the complete German Bible is published

1546

Dies in Eisleben, Germany, February 18; buried at the Castle Church, Wittenberg, Germany

1530

1540

1529

Pope Clemend VII refuses to grant England's King Henry VIII a divorce, setting the stage for England's separation from the Roman Catholic Church

1540

Spanish explorer Francisco Vasquez de Coronado leads an expedition into what is now the southwestern United States

DATE OF BIRTH: November 10, 1483

BIRTHPLACE: Eisleben, Germany

FATHER: Hans Luder (1459–1530)

MOTHER: Margarethe Luder (1460–1531)

EDUCATION: Latin schools at Mansfield and Magdeburg

St. George's Latin school in Eisenach

University of Erfurt

SPOUSE: Katharina von Bora (1499–1552)

DATE OF MARRIAGE: June 13, 1525

CHILDREN: Hans (1526–?)
Elizabeth (1527–1528)
Magdalena (1529–1542)
Martin Jr. (1531–1565)
Paul (1533–1593)
Margarethe (1534–1570)

DATE OF DEATH: February 18, 1546

PLACE OF BURIAL: Castle Church, Wittenberg, Germany

FURTHER READING

Crompton, Samuel Willard. *Martin Luther.* Broomall, Pa.: Chelsea House, 2004.

MacDonald, Fiona. *The Reformation*. Austin, Texas: Raintree Steck-Vaughn, 2002.

Mullett, Michael A., and Jeff Edwards. *The Reformation*. Crystal Lake, Ill.: Rigby Interactive Library, 1996.

van Rijswijk, Cor. *Martin Shows the Way.* Neerlandia, Alberta: Inheritance Publications, 2004.

LOOK FOR MORE SIGNATURE LIVES
BOOKS ABOUT THIS ERA:

Desiderius Erasmus: *Writer and Christian Humanist*
ISBN 0-7565-1584-X

Pope Leo X: *Opponent of the Reformation*
ISBN 0-7565-1594-7

Catherine de Medici: *The Power Behind the French Throne*
ISBN 0-7565-1581-5

William Tyndale: *Bible Translator and Martyr*
ISBN 0-7565-1599-8

ON THE WEB

For more information on *Martin Luther*, use FactHound.

1. Go to *www.facthound.com*
2. Type in a search word related to this book or this book ID: 0756515939
3. Click on the *Fetch It* button.

FactHound will fetch the best Web sites for you.

HISTORIC SITES

Castle Church
Wittenberg, Germany
Where Martin Luther preached and posted his *Ninety-Five Theses*

Eisleben, Germany
Where Martin Luther was born, preached his last sermon, and died

communion
a Christian rite in which consecrated bread and wine are taken to remember Christ's sacrifice on the cross

edict
a formal proclamation issued by a ruler

excommunicate
to exclude a church member from participating in Mass and other rites of the Catholic Church

heresy
a belief that goes against established religious teachings

indulgence
document signed by the pope that is said to shorten a person's time in purgatory

Mass
a Roman Catholic religious service

ordain
to formally admit a person into the clergy

penance
acts that prove people are sorry for their sins

pilgrimage
a journey to a holy place, undertaken for religious reasons

purgatory
a place where Catholics believe that souls of the dead suffer for a time to cleanse their sins before entering heaven

sacrament
a holy rite in a Christian church, such as baptism, communion, or confession

Chapter 1

Page 9, line 13: Patrick Collinson.*The Reformation: A History*. New York: Modern Library, 2004, p. 19.

Page 10, line 24: Ibid., p. 28.

Page 13, line 13: James M. Kittelson. *Luther the Reformer: The Story of the Man and His Career*. Minneapolis: Fortress Press, 1986, p. 160.

Page 13, line 18: Ibid.

Page 14, line 4: *The Reformation: A History*, p. 63.

Page 14, line 11: *Luther the Reformer: The Story of the Man and His Career*, p. 161.

Chapter 3

Page 25, line 5: Martin Marty. *Martin Luther*. New York: Viking Penguin, 2004, pp. 6–7.

Page 28, line 14: Roland H. Bainton. *Here I Stand: A Life of Martin Luther*. New York: Penguin Books, 1977, p. 30.

Page 28, line 24: Ibid., p. 31.

Page 30, line 5: Frederick Nohl. *Luther: Biography of a Reformer*. St. Louis, Mo.: Concordia Publishing House, 2003, p. 34.

Page 32, line 10: *Luther the Reformer: The Story of the Man and His Career*, p. 59.

Page 35, line 8: Ibid., p. 60.

Page 35, line 15: *Here I Stand: A Life of Martin Luther*, p. 37.

Page 36, line 8: *Martin Luther*, p. 13.

Page 36, line 27: *Here I Stand: A Life of Martin Luther*, p. 43.

Page 37, line 10: *Luther the Reformer: The Story of the Man and His Career*, p. 83.

Page 39, line 18: Ibid., p. 95.

Page 40, line 1: Ibid., p. 100.

Page 40, line 8: The Literature Network. 08 Dec. 2005. www.online-literature.com/bible/Romans/

Page 40, line 16: Martin Luther. *Luthers Werke in Auswahl*. 6th ed. Volume 4. (trans. Andrew Thornton). Berlin: de Gruyter, 1967, pp. 421–429. 18 Nov. 2005. www.iclnet.org/pub/resources/text/wittenberg/luther/tower.txt.

Chapter 4

Page 44, line 25: *Luther the Reformer: The Story of the Man and His Career*, p. 103.

Page 45, line 7: Ibid., pp. 103–104.

Page 46, line 17: Timothy F. Lull. *Martin Luther's Basic Theological Writings*. Minneapolis: Fortress Press, 1989, p. 21.

Page 47, line 4: Ibid., p. 26.

Page 48, line 8: Ibid., p. 28.

Page 49, line 1: *Luther the Reformer: The Story of the Man and His Career*, p. 107.

Page 49, line 21: "Martin Luther: The Reluctant Revolutionary." 18 Nov. 2005. www.pbs.org/empires/martinluther.

Chapter 5

Page 53, line 2: *Luther the Reformer: The Story of the Man and His Career*, p. 112.

Page 56, line 1: Ibid., p. 123.

Page 56, line 11: Ibid., p. 124.

Page 56, line 15: Ibid.

Chapter 6

Page 65, line 11: John M. Todd. *Luther: A Life*. New York: Crossroads Publishing, 1982. 18 Nov. 2005. www.religion-online.org/showchapter. asp?title=801&C=1064.

Page 66, line 10: *Luther: Biography of a Reformer*, p. 100.

Page 67, line 9: *Luther the Reformer: The Story of the Man and His Career*, p. 161.

Page 68, line 8: Ibid.

Page 68, line 11: *Martin Luther*, p. 68.

Chapter 7

Page 72, line 11: Ibid., p. 71.

Chapter 8

Page 82, line 2: *Luther the Reformer: The Story of the Man and His Career*, p. 201.

Page 84, line 3: "Katharina von Bora (1499–1552)." *Reformation Tours*. 18 Nov. 2005. www. reformationtours.com/site/490868/page204052.

Page 84, line 7: Ibid.

Page 85, line 10: "A Mighty Fortress Is Our God: Martin Luther." 18 Nov. 2005. www.luther.de/en.

Page 86, line 15: *Luther the Reformer: The Story of the Man and His Career*, p. 234.

Chapter 9

Page 89, line 13: *Martin Luther*, p. 128.

Page 90, line 16: Ibid., p. 143.

Page 90, line 21: Ibid., p. 144.

Page 91, line 6: "Martin Luther." 18 Nov. 2005. http://en.wikipedia.org/wiki/Martin_Luther.

Page 92, line 4: Ibid.

Page 92, sidebar: "A Christian Sermon Over the Body and at the Funeral of the Venerable Dr. Martin Luther, Preached by Mr. Johann Bugenhagen Pomeranus, Doctor and Pastor of the Churches in Wittenberg." *The Lewis H. Beck Center for Electronic Collections & Services*. 08 Dec. 2005. http://chaucer.library.emory.edu/luther/luther_site/luther_text.html.

Page 95, line 12: *Martin Luther*, p. 188.

Bainton, Roland H. *Here I Stand: A Life of Martin Luther.* New York: Penguin Books, 1977.

Collinson, Patrick. *The Reformation: A History.* New York: Modern Library, 2004.

Dillenberger, John., ed. *Martin Luther: Selections From His Writings.* Garden City, N.Y.: Doubleday, 1961.

"Katharina von Bora (1499–1552)." *Reformation Tours.* 18 Nov. 2005. www.reformationtours.com/site/490868/page/204052.

Kittelson, James M. *Luther the Reformer: The Story of the Man and His Career.* Minneapolis: Fortress Press, 1986.

Lull, Timothy F. *Martin Luther's Basic Theological Writings.* Minneapolis: Fortress Press, 1989.

Luther, Martin. *Luthers Werke in Auswahl.* Volume 4. 6th ed. (trans. Andrew Thornton). Berlin: de Gruyter, 1967. 18 Nov. 2005. www.iclnet.org/pub/resources/text/wittenberg/luther/tower.txt

"Martin Luther's Sermons." 18 Nov. 2005. www.trinitylutheranms.org/MartinLuther/SermonsPage.html

"Martin Luther: The Reluctant Revolutionary." 18 Nov. 2005. www.pbs.org/empires/martinluther.

Marty, Martin. *Martin Luther.* New York: Viking Penguin, 2004.

"A Mighty Fortress Is Our God." HymnSite.com. 18 Nov. 2005. www.hymnsite.com/lyrics/umh110.sht.

"A Mighty Fortress Is Our God: Martin Luther." 18 Nov. 2005. www.luther.de/en.

Nohl, Frederick. *Luther: Biography of a Reformer.* St Louis, Mo.: Concordia Publishing House, 2003.

Peterson, Susan Lynn. "The Life of Martin Luther." 18 Nov. 2005. www.susan-lynnpeterson.com/luther/home.html.

"Project Wittenberg: Lutheran Electronic Archive." 18 Nov. 2005. www.ctsfw.edu/etext/luther.

"Romans." The Literature Network. 08 Dec. 2005. www.online-literature.com/bible/Romans.

Smith, Preserved. *The Life and Letters of Martin Luther.* New York: Barnes & Noble, 1911 (reprint 1968).

Todd, John M. *Luther: A Life.* New York: Crossroad Publishing, 1982. 18 Nov. 2005. www.religion-online.org/showchapter.asp?title=801&C=1064.

"Writings of Martin Luther." *Internet Sacred Text Archive.* 18 Nov. 2005. www.sacred-texts.com/chr/luther.

Barbara A. Somervill has been writing for more than 30 years. She has written newspaper and magazine articles, video scripts, and books for children. She enjoys writing about science and investigating people's lives for biographies. Somervill lives with her husband in South Carolina.

Image Credits

The Granger Collection, New York, cover (top), 4–5, 12, 14, 52, 100 (top left); Stock Montage/Getty Images, cover (bottom), 2, 24, 26, 59, 96 (top right), 97 (top); Bettmann/Corbis, 8, 45, 62, 84; Hulton Archive/Getty Images, 10, 75, 78, 100 (bottom); Private Collection/The Bridgeman Art Library, 11, 61, 99 (top right); Mary Evans Picture Library, 16, 21, 33, 37, 38, 50, 55, 57, 64, 72, 79, 82, 96 (top left), 98 (top left), 99 (top, left and middle); Sammlungen auf der Wartburg, Eisenach, Germany/The Bridgeman Art Library, 18, 19; Library of Congress, 22, 96 (bottom left), 97 (bottom), 99 (bottom), 101 (bottom, all); National Gallery of Scotland, Edinburgh, Scotland/The Bridgeman Art Library, 27; Courtesy of Hans Rollmann, image from Luthers Leben by Julius Köstlin (Leipzig: Fues's Verlag [R. Reisland], 1889), 29; Arte & Immagini srl/Corbis, 31; Scala/Art Resource, N.Y., 34; Stock Montage, 41; North Wind Picture Archives, 42, 98 (top right); Stapleton Collection/Corbis, 44; Snark/Art Resource, N.Y., 47; Summerfield Press/Corbis, 48; Hulton-Deutsch Collection/Corbis, 67; Erich Lessing/Art Resource, N.Y., 70; Vanni Archive/Corbis, 76; David Lees/Corbis, 80, 100 (top right); Corbis, 87, 101 (top left); H. Lange/zefa/Corbis, 88; Dave Bartruff/Corbis, 93, 101 (top right); James L. Amos/Corbis, 95; Wildside Press, 96 (bottom right); Corel, 98 (bottom).